A+
books

T0044878

A Day in the Life of a
POLAR BEAR
A 4D BOOK

by Sharon Katz Cooper

Consultant: Robert T. Mason
Professor of Integrative Biology
J.C. Braly Curator of Vertebrates
Oregon State University

PEBBLE
a capstone imprint

Download the Capstone 4D app!

- Ask an adult to download the Capstone 4D app.
- Scan the cover and stars inside the book for additional content.

When you scan a spread, you'll find
fun extra stuff to go with this book!
You can also find these things
on the web at www.capstone4D.com
using the password: polarbear.15169

A+ Books are published by Pebble
1710 Roe Crest Drive, North Mankato, Minnesota 56003
www.mycapstone.com

Copyright © 2019 by Pebble, a Capstone imprint. All rights reserved. No part of this publication
may be reproduced in whole or in part, or stored in a retrieval system, or transmitted in any form
or by any means, electronic, mechanical, photocopying, recording, or otherwise, without written
permission of the publisher.

Cataloging-in-Publication data is available on the Library of Congress website.
ISBN 978-1-5435-1516-9 (library binding)
ISBN 978-1-5435-1520-6 (paperback)
ISBN 978-1-5435-1524-4 (eBook PDF)
Summary: It's morning on the tundra. Time to start the day up close with a
polar bear! Give young nature explorers and zoologists an exciting way to learn
about the icy homes, physical features, and behaviors of this Arctic bear by
following it throughout one day.

Editorial Credits
Gina Kammer editor; Jennifer Bergstrom, designer;
Morgan Walters, media researcher; Laura Manthe, production specialist

Photo Credits
Alamy: John Schwieder, 5; Getty Images: Daniel J. Cox, 17; iStockphoto: Andyworks, 8; Newscom:
Design Pics / Richard Wear, 18; Shutterstock: Alexey Seafarer, 7, 16, Christopher Wood, 4, 21, City
Escapes Nature Photo, 25, dangdumrong, 13, FloridaStock, 10, GUDKOV ANDREY, 6, Heather M
Davidson, 24, Jjo Crebbin, 12, Joshua Haviv, 11, Lamberrto, 19, MuchMania, Cover, design element
throuout, MyImages - Micha, 9, NaturesMomentsuk, 23, 26, Ondrej Prosicky, 1, 30, outdoorsman,
29, rbrown10, Cover, Richard Seeley, 14, robert mcgillivray, 22, Sergey Uryadnikov, 20, 27, Shvaygert
Ekaterina, 15

Note to Parents, Teachers, and Librarians

This book uses full color photographs and a nonfiction format to introduce the concept of a polar
bear's day. *A Day in the Life of a Polar Bear* is designed to be read aloud to a pre-reader or to be read
independently by an early reader. Photographs help listeners and early readers understand the text
and concepts discussed. The book encourages further learning by including the following sections:
Table of Contents, Glossary, Read More, Internet Sites, Critical Thinking Questions, and Index. Early
readers may need assistance using these features.

TABLE OF CONTENTS

A Polar Bear's Day

The polar bear opens her eyes. Her two cubs open their eyes too. All three bears stretch and go out of their den. The little snow cave keeps them warm and safe in the cold Arctic.

The hungry mother bear lifts her 400-pound (181-kilogram) body from the ground. She is a carnivore. She eats other animals.

HUNGRY!

Today she will show her cubs how to hunt. She is a predator.

The bear looks white in the sunlight. Her fur helps her blend in with the snow. She is hard for her prey to see! But her fur isn't really white. It's clear. Each hair is hollow.

Black skin lies beneath the fur. The dark color soaks up sunlight and keeps the bear's body warm.

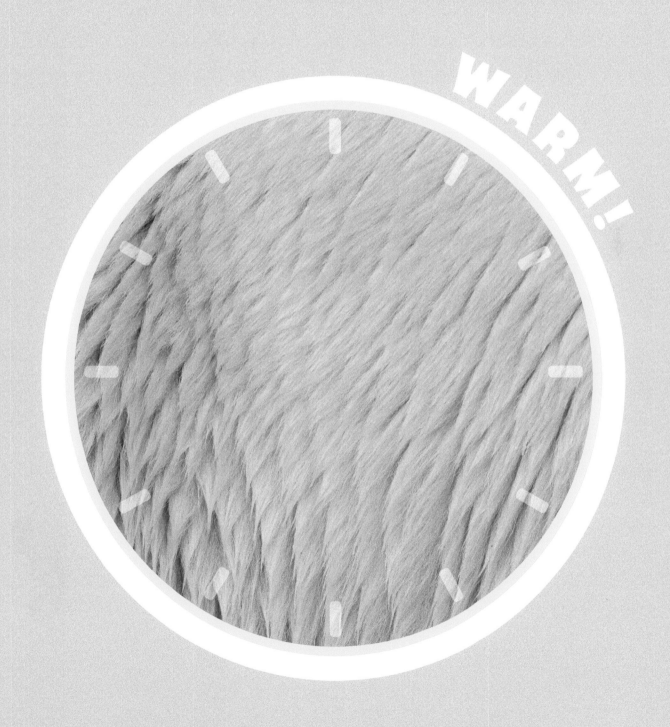

WARM!

At the edge of the ice, the bear jumps into the water. *SPLASH! SWISH!*

SPLASH!

The polar bear is a good swimmer. She hunts for a fat, tasty seal. Her cubs stay on the ice nearby and watch.

The water is very cold, but the bear does not mind. She has a thick layer of blubber and fur to keep her warm. Her oily fur pushes water away.

After a few hours, she pulls herself out of the water. She shakes the water off quickly. If she doesn't, ice will form on her body.

13

There! What's that? It's a seal lying on the ice. The polar bear lunges! She bites the seal, kills it, and drags it to her cubs.

SEAL!

14

Time to eat! The fat seal will feed the bear's family for more than a week.

Now it's time to go home. The polar bear and her cubs rest. She feeds them milk from her body.

Then she licks their fur. It's a bear cub bath!

LICK!

After their bath, the cubs play. They chase each other in circles. They climb on their mother. She rolls in the snow.

The bear is on her back. Her paws are in the air. Her cubs jump and play around her.

19

YIP! The polar bear hears a noise. She sees something move.

YIP!

She stands tall on two back feet to check for danger. She is not afraid for herself. Nothing would try to eat an adult polar bear. She is too big and fierce! She worries only for her cubs.

CHUFF, CHUFF, CHUFF! the bear calls. It's a fox! The bear drops to all fours and runs toward it. She can run about 25 miles (40 kilometers) per hour if she needs to.

FOX!

The bear has thick pads on the bottom of her feet. They have little bumps on them. Hair grows between these pads and the bear's toes.

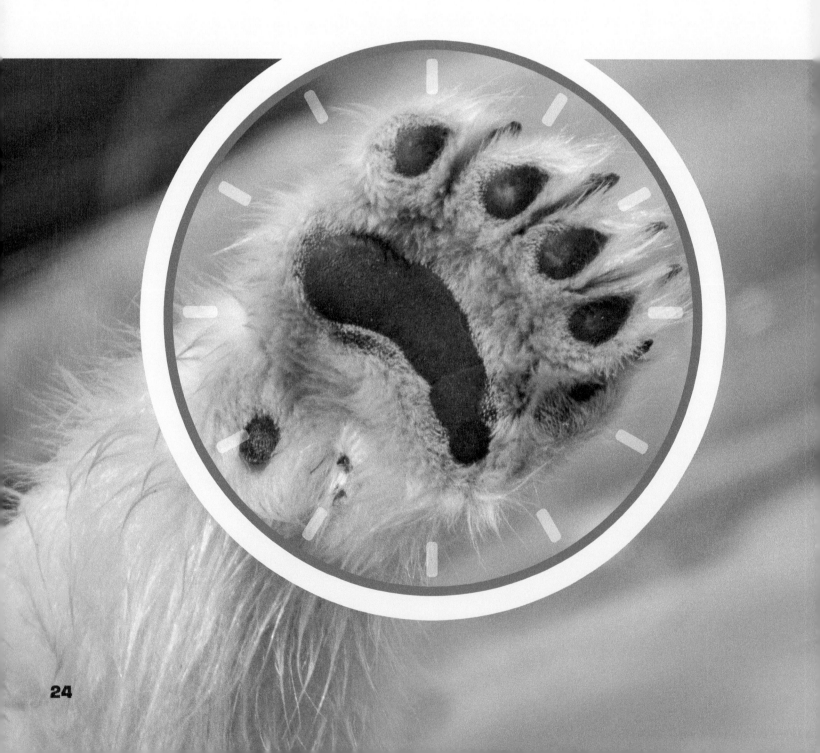

The pads and hair keep her from slipping on the snow and ice as she runs.

The fox quickly runs away. He is no match for a grown polar bear. She is very strong. One hit with her paw could kill the fox.

At the end of the day, the polar bear and her cubs snuggle in their den. Their body heat keeps them warm. The bear gives milk to her cubs. When they are full, they fall asleep. And so does she.

Goodnight, polar bear!

LIFE CYCLE OF A
POLAR BEAR

1
Polar bear cubs are born from November to January. There are usually **TWO** in a litter.

2
Polar bear cubs weigh about **16** to **24 OUNCES** (454 to 680 grams) and are about **12 INCHES** (30 centimeters) long.

3
After about **TWO AND A HALF YEARS,** young bears are on their own.

4
Females find a mate at **4** to **5 YEARS** old.

5
It takes about **EIGHT MONTHS** for a cub to grow inside its mother. Females have new litters about every **THREE YEARS.**

6
Polar bears live for **15** to **25 YEARS.**

Glossary

blubber—a thick layer of fat under the skin of some animals; blubber keeps animals warm

carnivore—an animal that eats only meat

litter—a group of animals born at the same time to the same mother

mate—the male or female partner of an animal

oily—covered with a slippery liquid that does not mix with water

predator—an animal that hunts other animals for food

prey—an animal hunted by another animal for food

Read More

Carrington, Stephanie. *Huge Polar Bears*. Great Big Animals. New York: Gareth Stevens Publishing, 2018.

Schuh, Mari C. *Polar Bears*. Black and White Animals. North Mankato, Minn: Capstone Press, 2017.

Ward, Finn. *Polar Bears at the Zoo*. Zoo Animals. New York: Gareth Stevens Publishing, 2016.

Internet Sites

Use FactHound to find Internet sites related to this book.

Visit *www.facthound.com*

Just type in 9781543515169 and go.

Super-cool stuff!

Check out projects, games and lots more at
www.capstonekids.com

Critical Thinking Questions

1. How do you think the polar bear's skin and fur help it in the cold Arctic?

2. Why do you think the polar bear hunts?

3. How does the polar bear protect her cubs from danger?

Index